Bible Application

Skits Kids CanDo

24 Quick and Easy Scripts for Ages 8 to 12

STANDARD PUBLISHING

Cincinnati, Ohio

Bible Application Skits Kids Can Do

Standard Publishing, Cincinnati, Ohio
A division of Standex International Corporation
© 1999 Standard Publishing
All rights reserved
Printed in the United States of America

Cover and inside design: Diana Walters
Graphic layout: Dale Meyers
Editor: Heather Turner
Acquisitions editors: Lise Caldwell, Ruth Frederick

06 05 04 03 02 01   5 4 3

ISBN: 0-7847-1075-9

Contents

Introduction

Bible Application Skits Kids Can Do is an easy-to-use children's ministry resource designed to help teach children important Bible themes and concepts. Each skit takes minimal planning and rehearsal, and many skits involve your entire group. The following are tips on how to use the audience participation activities with groups of various sizes, as well as rehearsal tips and simple memorization pointers.

Usage Guide for Large and Small Groups

These skits can be used by groups of 20 or 200! We want to help you adapt these skits to fit your own situation. Each skit has a section called Scene Setup. As you read through Scene Setup, here are some directions for specific circumstances.

Groups of 25 or Fewer

Often there is a role for all/some of your children. You will use all your children in these parts. Direction given for positioning the characters refer to the performance area. You will use the room itself as the performance area.

Often there is no audience, and the action of the drama will take place right in the middle of all the children. Any suggestions for audience participation will be performed by all the children.

Groups of 25 or more

Often there is a role for all/some of your children. You will use some of your children. Directions given for positioning the characters refer to the performance area. If you do not have an actual stage, you will designate a portion of your room to be the performance area, with the remaining children forming the audience.

There may be suggestions for audience participation. For example, the audience may be asked to join some of the children on the stage in chanting a refrain or making specific sound effects. Consider each script to determine whether or not it is practical for all the children to join in.

Also stay alert for roles that can be divided and assigned to more than one child. For instance, you may use two or three narrators instead of only one. This not only involves more children in active participation, but also reduces the amount of memorization required by any one child. And remember, many roles can be either male or female with a simple change of a name!

Rehearsal and Memorization Tips

Involve as many interested children as you can as primary actors. While a few roles may call for a strong, charismatic actor, most of them do not. Encourage children who are reluctant to give acting a try, but never force an unwilling child to get on stage.

Give your actors the script a week or two in advance, if possible. Have them read it out loud. Explain any words or concepts with which they are unfamiliar. It is difficult to memorize something you don't understand! Provide highlighters for each actor to highlight her part.

Read the Scripture verse or passage out loud. Consider giving a brief lesson or devotional on the topic. Ask your actors if they identify with the story or struggle. How?

Now have the actors read the script aloud again. This time have them act out the scene. Tell them when to stand, sit, walk, enter, and exit. Encourage them to write these instructions on their photocopy of the script. If anyone seems to be struggling with meaning or pronunciation, clarify it for him.

Instruct your actors to look at their scripts every day. They should

• Read the script several times straight through, then try to summarize the story line in their own words.

• Read it through again, this time covering their own lines, trying to remember them as they go.

• Once they are able to do this, have them ask someone to read the lines out loud with them, allowing the actors to recite their own lines.

If a child finds memorization difficult, but wants to act, encourage him to record the entire script on a tape and listen to it frequently. Then he can record himself reading all the lines but his, leaving pauses for him to say his lines.

You will need one more rehearsal, which can be just before the performance, or at a separate time. Begin this rehearsal with a few silly tongue twisters or a goofy game, in the performance area if possible. This will help the children relax and begin to behave naturally in the performance space.

Then have them rehearse the scene. Encourage them to be relaxed, have fun, and speak naturally (and loudly). Emphasize that they should speak each word clearly and distinctly. Correct any blocking (stage movement) they may have missed or forgotten.

Before you perform, gather your actors and pray with them. Pray that they will remember their lines, remain calm, and help their peers understand the lesson. After the performance, remember to give positive feedback, especially to insecure or inexperienced actors.

Exhibit #101

Scripture
Genesis 1, 2

Props
chair

Characters
Museum Guide
Tourist One
Tourist Two
Tourist Three
Tourist Four
Ralph (non-speaking part)

Scene Setup
Place one chair in the middle of the performance area. Gather all/some of the children, including the five actors, at one end. When the skit begins, have the *Museum Guide* lead this group to where the chair is occupied by *Ralph*.

Say, "Field trip! We're going on a guided tour of a world-famous art museum. Follow along behind the *Museum Guide* and be sure not to touch any of the priceless works of art as you move through the galleries."

Script

Museum Guide: And now, please follow me as we go into the Central Gallery where the museum keeps the prize of the entire collection, Exhibit #101. Remember no flash pictures are permitted, and please do not touch any of the paintings, sculptures, or other objects of art on display. Ladies and gentlemen, behold the jewel of the museum's collection, Exhibit #101—Ralph! As you can see, Ralph is designed in the classic style by a master artist.

Tourist One: Excuse me, are you talking about this guy sitting here?

Museum Guide: Yes. This is Ralph.

Tourist Two: There's nothing special about this guy. I mean, he's sort of bald and kind of dumpy.

Tourist Three: Yeah. There are people who are stronger than this guy.

Tourist Four: People who are smarter.

Tourist One: And better dressed.

Tourist Two: Some of the paintings we've seen are worth fifty million dollars. You're telling me this Ralph guy is worth more than that?

Tourist One: Yeah. No offense, but even this guy's *suit* is cheap.

Museum Guide: You're right about the suit. And he does have a few flaws. Okay, he has a *lot* of flaws. But this piece of art is more valuable than any other in the museum.

Tourist Three: But why?

Museum Guide: Because Ralph was created by God. And God loved Ralph so much that God sent his only Son, Jesus, to save Ralph. What makes Ralph so valuable is that he was designed by God and paid for by God.

Tourist Four: Wow!

Museum Guide: And something else. You've been made by the same Creator, who paid the same price for you. You've been made by God in his own image.

Tourist One: So I'm a work of art, too! I'm priceless! I guess I should be safely locked away in a museum display case!

Tourist Two: You know, I was just thinking the same thing.

Digging Deeper

- How does it feel knowing you're created in God's image?
- What do you think it means to be created in God's image?
- How does it feel knowing God paid the price of his own Son for you?

Broken Promises

Scripture
Psalm 145:13

Props
none

Characters
Jack
Jill

Scene Setup
Jill sits on the floor looking over the heads of the audience as if she's waiting for something to happen. *Jack* waits 10 seconds and walks across performance area behind her as though he's walking down the sidewalk. *Jack* walks past *Jill*, pauses, then comes back to speak to her. Your audience will vote on the outcome of the skit.

Script

Jack: Hey—what'cha doing?

Jill: Waiting for Nancy.

Jack: Oh. How about if we talk while you wait?

Jill: Great. Pull up some curb.

Jack: You and Nancy going someplace?

Jill: No. Nancy promised to give me twenty-five dollars. She told me to wait for her here.

Jack: Oh. How long have you been waiting?

Jill: [*checks watch*] About two hours.

Jack: But Nancy lives right over there in that white house.

Jill: Yeah. Guess she had to look around her room or something.

Jack: Isn't Nancy the one who promised that she'd help you with that social studies project, and she never showed up?

Jill: Yes.

Jack: And isn't Nancy the one who promised that you could go with her family to Disney World? And then she said it wouldn't work out after all?

Jill: Well, yes.

Jack: So why do you think she'll keep this promise?

Jill: Ummm . . . Well . . .

Jack: Look, let's take a vote, okay? Everyone who thinks Nancy is going to come back with twenty-five dollars, raise your hand. [*pause while audience votes*] Everyone who thinks Nancy won't come back, raise your hand. [*pause while audience votes*]

Jill: [*counts votes*] Guess I'm wasting my time.

Jack: Not really—at least we got to talk. And if you come back to my house, my mom will give us both ice cream cones. Come on.

Jill: Really?

Jack: Yeah—I promise!

Jack *and* Jill *both walk off*

Digging Deeper

- Name a time when someone didn't keep a promise to you. How did you feel?
- Name a promise God has kept.
- What's one promise Jesus made to you that he hasn't yet kept? Do you think he'll keep it? Why or why not?

Table Talk

Scripture
Exodus 5–20

Props
two tables
tablecloth (optional)
three chairs

Characters
Flick
Flack
Prayer Person

Scene Setup
Seat *Flick* and *Flack* at a small table, as if in a restaurant. Place *Prayer Person* at a nearby table with one or two others.

Say, "It's dinnertime here at the elegant Le Shazaam Restaurant. Crystal goblets gleam in the candlelight. Expensive china and silver rest on a starched linen tablecloth. All of you are dressed in your very best finery. You've been seated and are now waiting for the arrival of your dinners. There's small talk all around the tables, but two of you have a particularly interesting conversation."

Script

flick:	Driving to the restaurant tonight I saw the worst accident. At least fifteen cars, a couple ambulances, lots of police cars.
flack:	That must have been horrible.
flick:	It certainly was. I was stuck in traffic almost thirty minutes. I'm lucky I wasn't late for dinner.
flack:	Well, I've had a terrible week, too. Tonight our limousine dropped us off several blocks from the restaurant. We thought we'd walk a bit for the exercise. Anyway, on the way here a homeless person stopped us to ask for money.
flick:	Oh, my. Were you scared?

Flack: No, but he smelled terrible. Don't homeless people ever bathe?

Flick: There ought to be a law. People can be so inconsiderate!

Flack: And this week the man who cleans our pool didn't show up. When we called to complain, his wife said he'd had a heart attack and was in the hospital. That's all very sad, but what about our pool? She could have at least had someone else do the job.

Flick: You've had a hard week, all right.

Prayer Person: Before our meal is served, would you join me in prayer?

Flack: We'll finish talking in just a moment.

Prayer Person: Dear Lord, thank you for taking such good care of us this past week. Especially for taking care of us in ways we didn't even notice. For all the accidents we haven't been in. For the sicknesses we haven't suffered. For our homes. For the good food we're about to enjoy. Thank you for all these blessings, and please be with people who don't have them. Give us opportunities to share in the coming week. Amen.

Flack: Of all the nerve! I can tell he hasn't had the terrible week we've had!

Digging Deeper

2 What are some blessings you've enjoyed the past week?

2 What ways has God cared for you that you didn't stop to notice at the time?

2 In what ways can God use you to help care for others?

Double Identity

Scripture
Luke 2:40-52

Props
crown

Characters
Mrs. McMillan
King Abudabu
Sarah
Todd

Scene Setup
Arrange some/all of the children in rows, as if they're seated at desks in school. Place *Mrs. McMillan* and *King Abudabu*, who is wearing the crown, in the front of the class. Place *Sarah* in the rows of students.

Say, "Welcome to Mrs. McMillan's class at school! Your teacher has finished a lesson about why birds migrate south for the winter, and now she wants to take care of some other business. Pay attention or you'll be headed for the principal's office!"

Script

Mrs. McMillan: Class, I want to introduce you to a new student. This is Abudabu, His Royal Highness, the king of Botaroon. Welcome to our class, Your Royal Highness.

King Abudabu: Thank you.

Mrs. McMillan: Does anyone have any questions for the king?

Sarah and Todd: I do! I do!

Mrs. McMillan: Yes, Sarah?

Sarah: Are you really a king?

King Abudabu: Yes, though my kingdom is far from here.

Todd: And even though you're a king, you're coming to school here?

King Abudabu: Yes.

Sarah: I don't buy it! You can't be a student *and* a king!

Mrs. McMillan: Sarah—don't be rude!

Sarah: I mean it. Maybe you look like a king with that crown on your head, but no way would a king go to school here. A king would live in a palace and have a tutor.

King Abudabu: But I am a king. And I am a student.

Todd: Believe me, no king would eat the food they serve in this cafeteria!

King Abudabu: Still, I'm a king. And a student.

Sarah: Then do something kingly. Declare this a national holiday so we can all take the day off from school. Or buy us a new computer lab. I don't believe you can be a king and a student here at the same time.

King Abudabu: Children, I'm a king and a student.

Mrs. McMillan: I think that's enough questions for now, children. Take out your math homework and let's see how you answered question number six. The question was, "If a train leaves Chicago and goes east at 60 miles an hour and at the same time a train leaves Paris and goes north at 20 miles an hour, how hot will it be in Boston when the cows come home?"

Digging Deeper

- Would a king attend your school? Why or why not?
- Jesus was a man and God's Son. Name something that happened that showed that Jesus was a man. Name something he did that showed that he was also God's Son.
- If you'd been there when Jesus was on earth, do you think you'd have recognized him as God's Son? Why or why not?

Believe It or Not!

Scripture
John 20:30, 31

Props
can of soup

Characters
Clerk
Nancy
Harry

Scene Setup
Choose a few children to line up single file facing the *Clerk*, as if they're waiting to check out of a grocery store. Place *Nancy* second in the line of customers and *Harry* at the back of the line. Give the can of soup to *Nancy*.

Say, "Sometimes when you're stuck in line at the grocery store, you hear some really interesting conversations. Listen to this one!"

Script

Clerk: That will be 84 cents. Thank you. We appreciate your business. Next, please.

Nancy: Just a minute. I'm trying to decide if I want to buy this paper.

Clerk: The one on the rack? The *National Inquisition*? It's a buck forty-nine.

Nancy: Do you know if the articles in here are really true?

Clerk: I'm just guessing, but I'll bet the story about Elvis being abducted by aliens and returning as a high-school English teacher in Kalamazoo has a few holes in it. So you gonna buy it, or what?

Harry: [*with irritation in his voice*] Hey, lady, hurry up. There's a line, you know!

Nancy: It's this article about a man who was blind and crippled suddenly being healed that interests me. One minute he's blind and crippled and the next minute he can see and walk.

Clerk: Maybe he was faking being blind and crippled.

Nancy: How could someone fake being blind and crippled for 20 years?

Harry: [*with more irritation*] Hey, lady! My Popsicles are melting back here!

Clerk: He probably had some kind of surgery. Or a transplant.

Nancy: Says here it was an instant healing.

Clerk: Couldn't have happened. Had to be faked.

Nancy: You know, it has happened before. I've read about it.

Clerk: Where'd you read that? Another issue of the *Inquisition*? You can't believe everything you read.

Harry: [*very annoyed*] Lady! Please! Just buy the paper!

Nancy: Actually, I read it in the Bible.

Clerk: Oh. Well, like I said, you can't believe everything you read. Next, please!

Digging Deeper

- Do you believe that Jesus really did heal people instantly? Why or why not?
- Which healing miracle of Jesus do you think was most amazing? Why?
- Do you know anyone you wish Jesus would heal? Pray for that person.

Who's the Loser?

Scripture
Luke 19:1-10

Props
chairs

Characters
Bud
Nancy
Lester

Scene Setup
Place chairs in rows to resemble the seating on a school bus. Place *Bud* and *Nancy* on opposite sides of the aisle, with an open chair next to each of them. Have some/all of the children fill in the rows.

Place *Lester* standing at the front of the "bus," looking for a seat. *Lester* may be dressed as a classic "nerd."

Say, "Riding on a school bus is a great way to test your popularity. If you're too new or too short or too tall or too skinny or fat or not smart enough or too smart or you stutter or you're having a bad hair day—nobody wants to sit with you. It's a wonder anyone gets to sit down at all! This morning a new guy has walked onto the bus. Everyone knows at once he's different, and nobody wants him to sit next to him! Let's see how finding a seat goes for this poor newcomer."

—— Script ——

Bud: Look! It's that new kid from Springfield. My dad sold his family a house.

Nancy: I hear he's some kind of computer wizard.

Bud: My dad said his whole family are like, social retards or something. He's probably into computers because nobody can stand him. I mean, look at the guy—his shirt-tail is hanging out. His hair looks like he combed it with a coat hanger. He can't even find a seat!

Nancy: Well, nobody is inviting him to sit down.

Bud: No duh! Who wants to sit next to a loser?

Nancy: I'll ask him to sit by me. Maybe he's a great guy when you get to know him.

Bud: Maybe he's even worse than he looks!

Nancy: Guess I'll find out. Hey—new guy! Come sit over here!

Bud: I can't believe this—are you nuts?

Lester: [*walking down aisle and sitting next to* Nancy] Thanks. I don't know anybody yet. We just moved here.

Nancy: I figured. My name's Nancy.

Lester: Lester. Lester Ficklebun.

Bud: [*under his breath, but loud enough to be heard*] Figures you'd have a name like that.

Nancy: Bud, be quiet! So did you move here because your dad or mom got a new job?

Lester: Not really. My dad just retired. And back in Springfield we were always getting reporters calling us.

Bud: Probably crime reporters.

Nancy: Bud—be quiet! So, Lester, do you miss your friends back in Springfield?

Lester: Not really. We keep in touch by e-mail.

Nancy: I don't know much about e-mail.

Lester: It's a pretty cool way to communicate with your friends. My dad and I wrote this e-mail-linking software that lets you stay in touch even if you're at a new computer. It works with—

Bud: Wait a minute—are you saying you and your dad wrote the "Finkle-twinkle Software"?

Lester: Yeah.

Bud: [*with excitement*] I bought that software last night! You can set up e-mail so it follows you to any computer, and you get it five times as fast! I'm gonna install it tonight—how about you come over and help?

Lester: No, thanks.

Bud: Why not? I thought you needed some new friends.

Lester: You only want to be my friend because I can do something for you. Nancy wants to be my friend just to be my friend. Nancy, maybe you and your family can come over to our house sometime for dinner?

Nancy: I think my family would like that. Hey—we're at school. Come on, I'll show you where to find your classroom.

Nancy, Lester, *and* Bud *get up and file off the bus*

Digging Deeper

꿈 Describe a friend of yours. What makes this person a good friend?

꿈 Jesus was a friend to people who weren't popular. Why do you think Jesus befriended people nobody else liked?

꿈 What does it mean to love your friends in the same way Jesus loves us? Name a way to do that.

Make a Run for It!

Scripture
Luke 3:2-14

Props
none

Characters
Coach
Laura
Lisa

Scene Setup
Before the skit begins, ask some/all of the children to stand in rows with at least three feet between them, as if they're going to do calisthenics.

Say, "Okay, class, it's time for gym. But none of those namby-pamby gym classes like table tennis or creative movement. This is hard-core, muscle-building, do-or-die calisthenics—and leading us is none other than the Meanest Gym Teacher in the World, Coach Arthur Rumpswat!"

Script

Coach *stands in front of the class, facing them.* Lisa *and* Laura *stand next to each other in the back row.*

Coach: Okay, listen up, you lily-livered, noodle-armed, scrawny-legged excuses for good health. It's my job to shape you up.

Laura: This guy sounds like an army drill instructor.

Lisa: What's that?

Laura: A drill instructor is a guy who teaches soldiers how to do push-ups and march and stuff.

Coach: All right—who's talking? Identify yourself!

Laura: I was talking, Sir.

Lisa: Me too. I didn't know it was against the rules.

Coach: Then let me explain the rules to you. I am in command here. You will remain silent unless I ask you to speak—and I will *not* ask you to speak. Why? Because you'll soon be so out of breath you will be *unable* to speak. Your lungs will feel like they're on fire. Your ribs will feel as if they are going to explode through your chests. You will suffer, ladies and gentlemen—but it's going to be worth it because you will be healthy.

Lisa: Can we make a run for it?

Laura: You mean escape? I'll be right behind you!

Coach: In a few minutes we'll leave for a brisk, refreshing 20-mile run. But first you will practice taking orders. We will be running through alligator-infested swamps. Between pools of quicksand. Past rattlesnakes. So it is very important you obey my every command immediately. All right—Attention! March in place! Now right face! Now left face! Now repent!

Lisa: What?

Coach: Cease marching! I said "repent," soldiers—so do it!

Laura: But Sir, we don't understand what you mean, Sir.

Lisa: Yeah. "Left" I understand. "Right" I understand. But "Repent" I don't understand.

Coach: Then listen up, because I'll explain this just once. "Repent" means to turn around. If you're going one way and you repent, that means you turn around and go the other way.

Lisa: And it's a good thing to repent, right?

Coach: Yes.

Lisa: Then I repent of our 20-mile hike! Follow me if you'd rather take a 20-minute nap!

Lisa *exits, with* Laura *behind her*

Digging Deeper

- People who repent turn away from the wrong they're doing and do what is right. What would repentance look like if someone was a liar? A thief? A bully?
- Tell about a time in your life when you repented.
- How did you feel when you repented?

Dying to Get Out of Here

Scripture
1 Corinthians 15:3-8

Props
none

Characters
Mr. Smith
Mrs. Johnson
Ms. Coffey

Scene Setup
Ask some/all of the children to sit in rows facing the front of the room, either in chairs or on the floor. You are creating the chapel of a funeral home.

Say, "I'm sorry to say that you are now at a funeral. A family friend, Mr. Johnson, died a few days ago, and we're here to pay our last respects. We sit quietly, hands folded, wearing our very best black clothing. But up in the corner of the room the widow, Mrs. Johnson, is talking with two employees from the funeral home. If we listen closely, we may be able to hear what they're saying."

Script

Mr. Smith, Ms. Coffey, *and Mrs. Johnson* stand in the front of the performance area

Mr. Smith: Yes, Mrs. Johnson, how may we be of service in this, your time of grief?

Mrs. Johnson: It's about my husband's funeral.

Mr. Smith: Yes, it's going very well, don't you agree? A tasteful, dignified service if I say so myself.

Mrs. Johnson: Well, I'm calling it off.

Ms. Coffey: You can't just call off a funeral!

Mrs. Johnson: Sure can. I was reading about Jesus in the Bible this morning, and I've got some concerns.

Ms. Coffey: You mean Jesus? As in God's Son, Jesus? Why would that give you concerns?

Mrs. Johnson: Well, I got to thinking. Jesus rose from the dead. What if my husband rises from the dead? Will I get my money back for the funeral? I looked at our contract and it doesn't say anything about a refund.

Mr. Smith: But Mrs. Johnson, that just doesn't happen! That's why it's not in the contract!

Mrs. Johnson: I called the Hansen-Jansen Funeral Home. They offered me a money-back guarantee if they bury my husband and he rises from the dead. They were very helpful. I want them to do the job.

Ms. Coffey: Mrs. Johnson, you're in grief. You're upset. You're not making sense.

Mrs. Johnson: Don't insult me! If you're not willing to stand behind your work, don't blame me! And to think I heard that people were dying to do business with you. Well, I'm dying to get out of here! Hmmpf! Come on everybody—we're going to the Hansen-Jansen Funeral Home. A couple of you men grab old Henry's coffin there. We'll need to bring that along.

Mrs. Johnson leaves. Everyone follows her off stage.

Ms. Coffey: You know, sometimes I hate this business.

Mr. Smith: You and me both, sister. You and me both.

Digging Deeper

- After he rose from the dead, Jesus appeared to many people. How do you think those people felt? Why?

- If you had seen the resurrected Jesus, what would you have said to him?

- What will you say to the resurrected Jesus today? He's listening when you pray!

Good Vibrations

Scripture
Psalm 23

Props
none

Characters
Brian
Travis
Mrs. Adams

Scene Setup
Ask some/all of the children to stand and practice walking in place. This involves lifting and lowering feet, but not actually moving ahead.

Say, "It's early on a Monday morning, and we're trudging off to Maplehill Elementary School. Along the way we have to cross a very busy street, but fortunately there's a crossing guard to shepherd us safely across. Let's get underway, walking slowly in place. Do whatever Brian and Travis do. And let's have a great, fun-packed day at school as we memorize the capitals of states we'll never visit."

Script

Brian and Travis *stand side by side in the center of the performance area.* Mrs. Adams *lies on the floor in front of* Brian *and* Travis

Brian:	So you're the new kid, right? Your family moved into the old Herrik place?
Travis:	Yeah. This is my first day going to this school.
Brian:	Thought so. Look, stick with me and I'll show you all the shortcuts.
Travis:	Great. Thanks a lot.
Brian:	First we gotta stop here. [Brian *and* Travis *stop walking*]
Travis:	Hey—what happened to that lady?
Brian:	Her? She's just doing her job. That's Mrs. Adams, the crossing guard.

Travis:	But she's asleep!
Brian:	No, she's just concentrating.
Travis:	I think she's dead.
Brian:	Look, this woman is a legend. Let her do her job.
Travis:	[*looks left and right*] But there aren't any cars coming. And she's lying there with her eyes closed.
Brian:	Look, you're new so I'll explain it to you. Mrs. Adams is listening for cars. She lies there hearing the vibrations of car tires turning a couple blocks away. That way she knows what's coming without having to look.
Travis:	Oh, I get it. This is a joke, right? She's listening for vibrations of car tires. Do I look stupid to you?
Brian:	Don't believe me? Okay, I'll show you. Oh, Mrs. Adams. Oh, Mighty Queen of the Crossing Guards.
Mrs. Adams:	What'cha want? I'm tracking vibrations on a Ford pickup.
Brian:	There's a new guy here who doesn't believe you're working.
Mrs. Adams:	Where do you live, new guy?
Travis:	101 Pennway Drive.
Mrs. Adams:	That's north a couple blocks.
Brian:	She's tuning in on the vibrations.
Travis:	You're out of your mind!
Mrs. Adams:	Let's see. Your father is just leaving for work. He's driving a 1978 Volkswagen bug that needs air in the back left tire. And I think the bug is . . . blue.
Travis:	Wow! That's amazing!
Brian:	Now do you see why she's such a great crossing guard?
Mrs. Adams:	Okay kids, all clear. You can cross the street.
Brian:	Thanks for keeping us safe, Mrs. Adams.

Mrs. Adams: No problem, kid.

Brian: [*signaling everyone to follow as he jumps over* Mrs. Adams] Come on everybody! Last one to school has to kiss the principal!

Digging Deeper

≈ If you had someone like Mrs. Adams watching out for you when you had to cross a busy street, would you feel safe? Why or why not?

≈ Psalm 23 says God is our shepherd. How does God watch out for us?

≈ In what ways do you see God protecting you and your family?

Hangin' Out

Scripture
Genesis 42–50

Props
none

Characters
Jenny
Jeff

Scene Setup
Ask *Jenny* and some/all of the children to sit on the floor. Place *Jeff* offstage so he can walk into the scene.

Ask children to practice chanting as if they're at a sit-in. Their chant: "The principal is a bum! The principal is a bum!" Rehearse several times and tell children to deliver their lines when prompted.

Say, "It's early in the morning and Jeff is taking his dog for a walk. As he passes by the school, he sees a bunch of children sitting in front of the main door. And they're not just hanging around talking—they're deliberately blocking the door so no one can possibly get in. And they're chanting something. The person in charge is his friend, Jenny, so he stops to see what's happening.

———— Script ————

Jenny stands and faces the group. Jeff walks in, pretending to walk a dog.

Jenny: [*cueing the children*] Okay, everyone! Say it with me: The principal is a bum! The principal is a bum! The principal is a bum!

Jeff: Hi, Jenny. Why are you all hangin' out here?

Jenny: We're not hanging out. We're having a sit-in. You know, we're sitting here blocking the school doors because the principal is being unfair and nasty, and we want everyone to know it.

Jeff: What did the principal do?

Jenny: You don't know? Where have you been living? Mars?

Jeff: So, tell me about it.

Jenny: You know how the basketball team booster club always sells popcorn during lunch time?

Jeff: Yeah . . .

Jenny: And how they always have three kinds of popcorn? Regular, caramel, and extra-butter?

Jeff: Yeah . . .

Jenny: Well, last Friday the principal decided they can't sell extra-butter popcorn any more.

Jeff: So what?

Jenny: So what?! If the principal can take away our right for extra-butter popcorn, what will she take away next? Freedom of speech? The right to a fair trial? We won't stand for it! That's why we're having a sit-in right here in front of the school doors.

Jeff: Jenny, have you talked with Principal Mullins about this?

Jenny: No, but it's too late to talk. We want action!

Jeff: Jenny, the principal got rid of the extra-butter popcorn because butter dripped onto the carpet in the lunchroom. The janitor couldn't get the stains out. That's the only reason.

Jenny: That's not our problem! We're sitting right here blocking this door until the principal gives in to our demands to bring back the extra-butter popcorn. Right, guys? [*leads chant*] The principal is a bum! The principal is a bum!

Jeff: Okay—but you'll be sittin' here awhile. It's Saturday morning.

Digging Deeper

- How has God worked through a principal or another person in authority to help you?

- How should you treat leaders you like? Leaders you don't like?

- If someone who is in charge makes a rule you don't like, what should you do?

How Long Is Forever?

Scripture
Genesis 1:1

Props
bag of peanuts

Characters
Dick
Jane

Scene Setup
Group some/all of the children into "cages" of animals at a zoo. Create "cages" of gorillas, lions, and giraffes. Ask the groups of children to practice their best impersonations, then to silently stay in character as they listen to the skit. A few other children can follow *Dick* and *Jane* through the zoo.

Say, "Time to visit the zoo! Let's make sure we can hear our two visitors as they wander through the zoo."

Script

Jane: You seem quiet. What are you thinking about?

Dick: About these animals. And God. And the universe.

Jane: Wow—I figured you were just thinking about where we're going for lunch.

Dick: Look at those gorillas. They're big and hairy and strong, but I don't think they're all that smart. [*tosses a few peanuts to the gorillas, gorillas do their impersonations*] And those giraffes. Don't they look strange? Skinny legs and long necks and knobby little heads. [*tosses a few peanuts to the giraffes, giraffes do their impersonations*] What do they think about all day long?

Jane: Maybe they wonder why we're so short.

Dick: Think about it, Jane. God created all these animals. Every one of them. And he created us. And he created the world, and time, and the universe. He created everything.

Jane: God's been busy.

Dick: That's just it—he did all this and it didn't finish him off! He's still around! He's still doing things! Things I can't even begin to understand! He'll always exist! Forever!

Jane: Does that bother you? Not understanding God, I mean?

Dick: Yeah, I guess it does. It's like those lions there. [*tosses a few peanuts to lions, lions do their impersonations*] They're strong. They're fierce. They're brave. But they're pretty much stupid, too. They don't understand what we understand. That's like us and God—we see him but we don't understand him. We don't understand about forever.

Jane: Look, I know you're thinking deep thoughts. But I'm hungry, and those lions don't look happy that you're calling them "stupid." I vote we go get lunch before they turn us into lunch.

Digging Deeper

ى Does it bother you that you don't understand everything about God? Why or why not?

ى What does "eternal" mean?

ى How do you feel knowing that God has no beginning and no end?

Hope Strikes Out

Scripture
1 Thessalonians 4:13-18

Props
chairs

Characters
Announcer
Kurt
Kate

Scene Setup
Place six chairs in a row in the performance area. Seat *Kurt* and *Kate* in this row and ask four children to fill the remaining chairs. Ask some children to sit on the floor in front of the children in the chairs. Congratulations! You've created a section of bleachers at the baseball game. Place the *Announcer* behind the row of chairs.

   Say, "Play ball! We're here at the baseball diamond, and the game is almost over. The score is tied and the crowd is excited! When it's time to cheer, cheer. When you're disappointed about what happened down on the ball field, go ahead and boo! But make sure to hear what *Kurt* and *Kate* are saying."

Script

Announcer: [*excitedly*] It's nail-biting time for the home crowd. We're in the bottom of the ninth inning, bases are loaded, two outs, and Niles Anderson is coming up to the plate.

Kurt: This is great! We're gonna win this game!

Kate: How can you be so sure? Anderson hasn't had a hit in four games.

Kurt: Well, on the pre-game show he promised he'd hit one out of the park. And now is the time!

Kate: I'm not sure you can predict something like that.

Kurt: Hey—he promised!

Announcer: It's a swing and strike one on Anderson.

Kate: They don't call him "Hole-in-the-Bat Anderson" for nothing.

Announcer: The ball comes in fast and low and it's strike two on Anderson.

Kurt: No problem. Still got one to go. [*calling*] Stay loose! You'll get it next time!

Kate: You really think he's going to hit a homer?

Kurt: Hey—I've got hope!

Kate: You've got a surprise coming. Anderson can't hit! He's never been able to hit!

Kurt: He promised, remember?

Kate: But, Kurt . . .

Announcer: Anderson steps up to the plate and the pitcher releases the ball—strike three! The game is over and the home team loses again.

Kurt: But he promised! [*starts to whimper and cry*]

Kate: Kurt, he promised something he couldn't deliver. I know you're sad we lost and everything, but it's just a game. Don't worry about it. Every team loses now and then. You can always hope for a better game next time.

Kurt: I don't care about the team losing. I'm just sad 'cause now I gotta go home. My mom said if the team won I could go to the dairy whip and celebrate. But now, it's straight home—and it's my night to clean out the cat box!

Digging Deeper

↳ Jesus made some promises about taking his followers to heaven. Do you think Jesus can deliver on that promise? Why or why not?

↳ What does it mean to place your hope in Jesus?

↳ When you place your hope in Jesus, do people tell you you've made a good decision or a bad one? Why?

Follow the Leader

Scripture
1 Samuel 16, 17

Props
none

Characters
Director
Trumpet Player
Percussion Player

Scene Setup
Arrange some/all of the children in chairs in a semicircle as if they're in an orchestra. Assign the following roles to the children: Drums, Tubas, Violins, and Trumpets. Ask children to practice making noises like their instruments, using only their mouths. Place the *Director* in front of them.

Say, "Wonderful! Bravo! You are the world famous Royal Philharmonic Brandenburg Orchestra. Tonight is opening night of the Christmas program!"

Script

Trumpet: Excuse me. Could we talk with you, Director?

Director: Sure, but make it quick. The concert starts in just a few minutes.

Trumpet: It's just that, well, some of us were talking and we're not sure we need you.

Director: You don't need me?

Percussion: Yeah. I mean, we've got the music right in front of us.

Trumpet: Exactly. And we're all professional musicians.

Percussion: And all you do is wave that little white stick and look at us.

Trumpet: So we were thinking we'd just do the concert without you. On our own.

Director: I see. Well, if that's your decision. But may I make one suggestion? That you give it a try first? So you're sure?

Trumpet: No harm in that, I guess. Okay everybody, when I say "go," play "Silent Night." Ready, set, go!

Children in "orchestra" make a racket

Trumpet: Hold it! Hold it! What are you doing? You're not following my lead!

Percussion: Your lead? Everybody is supposed to be following my lead!

Trumpet: Except you can't keep a beat, you overstuffed bongo player!

Percussion: Me? You—you—you tasteless tooter!

Director: Silence, please! Silence! Is everyone happy with how your experiment turned out?

Percussion: Well, not exactly. After hearing how we sound without you, I'm thinking maybe we need a Director after all. Someone to get us working together.

Director: That's my job. I keep you all on beat, focused, and working together. Ladies and gentlemen, the curtain goes up in one minute. Everyone ready? Yes, Trumpet Number 1?

Trumpet: Can I at least try waving the little white stick sometime?

Director: It's called a baton, and no—you might hurt yourself.

Digging Deeper

- In what ways is Jesus a director for us?
- What would we be like if we quit listening to Jesus and obeying him?
- How has Jesus directed your actions in the last week?

Winner Takes All

Scripture
Psalm 147:5

Props
none

Characters
Mike
Andy
Ref

Scene Setup
Imagine the performance area as a wrestling ring, with a row of six children sitting "ringside" and the *Ref* in the middle of the ring. Place four children and *Mike* and *Andy* on the far side of the "ring," so that they face the audience.

Say, "It was tough getting tickets, but here you are: ringside at the wrestling match of the year. Up for grabs is the Heavyweight Championship Belt of the International Wrestling Federation. The match will begin in just a few moments."

———— Script ————

Mike: This is great, man! Ringside! This is so cool!

Andy: Yeah! We're so close that when the wrestlers sweat, it'll fly out and hit us!

Mike: Maybe this isn't so cool.

Ref: Ladies and gentlemen. Welcome to the match of the millennia! The fight to the finish! The war to end all wars! The winner-takes-all, no-holds-barred contest to determine who will carry home the gold Heavyweight Championship Belt! In this corner [*pointing to one corner of the ring*] we have the defending World Champion. At 315 pounds, Dr. Destructo, the Mauler from Montana!

Andy: Look at the size of that guy! He's got biceps bigger than my head!

Mike: He's got biceps bigger than your whole body!

Ref: And in this corner we have the challenger. At 325 pounds, the former German Grand Champion and three-time Mr. World title holder, Leopold Litz, the Munich Meatgrinder!

Andy: Leopold? What kind of name is Leopold for a wrestler?

Mike: You got a problem with it, you tell him!

Andy: These guys are so big. They're so powerful!

Mike: Nah, they aren't so tough. I know someone who could take them both.

Andy: Are you nuts? It would take an army to stop either one of those guys. Dr. Destructo can juggle Volkswagens! The Munich Meatgrinder got pulled over for a traffic ticket and he ate the policeman alive!

Mike: Still, he could take them.

Andy: Name someone who could handle these guys.

Mike: God.

Andy: God is a wrestler?

Mike: No, but he made those guys. He made the entire universe. He's more powerful than anything or anybody. He could take those guys.

Andy: I hope you're right, because I don't think they like us talking about them. They're coming over here and they don't look happy!

Mike: Run!

Mike and Andy run off stage

Digging Deeper

 ﹖ Tell about the most powerful person you've ever seen. Who was it? Why do you think the person is powerful?

 ﹖ Is there a limit to God's power? Why or why not?

 ﹖ What's an example of God's power?

He's All Ears

Scripture
Psalm 139:4-6

Props
chairs

Characters
Teacher
Jan
Dan

Scene Setup
Arrange rows of chairs so some/all of the children are seated as if they're in a traditional school. Place one child in each chair. Place the *Teacher* in the front of the class, and *Jan* and *Dan* in the back rows of the class.

   Say, "Welcome to Mr. Wazniak's class. You know those teachers who seem to be able to read minds and know everything? Well, this is one of those teachers—maybe. Today two of your classmates will find out. Your job is this: When the teacher asks you to respond to the question out loud, do so—all at once. No waiting for turns. No holding up your hands. Let's join class now."

Script

Teacher: I'm hoping you all read the homework assignment for today. Important stuff, American history! Now let's find out who came prepared. Jan?

Jan: Is this a quiz?

Teacher: Yes—but not a written one. I'll ask a question and you all answer out loud. I'll listen.

Dan: You mean all of us talk at once?

Teacher: Sure. Here's your first question: Who was the most important American president and why? At the count of three, shout out your answers but speak for no more than 10 seconds. One, two, three, go! *[students respond]* Hmm . . . Some of you didn't give very good reasons for picking your president. Yes, Jan?

Jan: Are you saying you heard all of our answers? At the same time?

Teacher: Yes. Though your saying Harrison Ford was the most important American president is an answer I wish I hadn't heard. He's an actor who played the president, Jan. Try to do better on the next question.

Jan: Wow—he actually heard me!

Dan: No way. He must be faking.

Jan: Then how did he know I said Harrison Ford?

Dan: Look, when he asks the next question I'll say he's ugly and see if he catches me.

Teacher: Class, please call out the name of a city you'd love to visit in America. One, two, three, go! [*students respond*] Jan, go to the principal's office this minute! I do not have ears like a donkey!

Jan: But I didn't say that!

Teacher: Don't argue with me, Jan. I know what I heard and I know your voice. Go see the principal.

Jan: But this isn't fair! I'm innocent! [*to* Dan] This is your fault! How did you do it?

Dan: [*in a "girl's" voice*] Have a good time at the principal's office!

Digging Deeper

↝ Do you believe God can hear when thousands of people pray at the same time? Why or why not?

↝ Why would a perfect God want to hear from imperfect people like us?

↝ How do you feel knowing God listens to you when you pray?

Jesus, Name Above All Names

Scripture
Isaiah 9:6

Props
music stands (optional)
art (optional)
overhead projector (optional)

Characters
Group One (three to five children)
Group Two (three to five children)
Group Three (remaining children)

Scene Setup
This skit is a Readers Theater, which means the children will read the script aloud together. Select a few children each to be in *Group One* and *Group Two*. Place them in the performance area. The rest of the children will form *Group Three*. Ask children in *Group One* and *Group Two* to practice reading aloud at a measured pace, projecting their voices so they're heard. Provide the readers in *Group One* and *Group Two* with music stands on which to place their scripts if possible. Teach *Group Three* its line. If possible, project the line overhead when it is time for them to deliver it. Explain that the script is Scripture and should be delivered with respect. This reading can be effective when presented with minimal staging, but you may wish to consider visual aids, such as motions or even paintings by the children representing different qualities of Christ.

Say, "What's in a name? In Jesus' time, a name was very important. Sometimes people changed their names or the names of others to reflect something about a person. Jesus had many names—and each of them tell us something about him."

Script

Group One: For unto us a child is born, to us a son is given.

Group Two: And the government will be on his shoulders.

Group Three: He is Jesus Christ, the Son of God.

Group One: He will be called Wonderful Counselor, Mighty God.

Group Two: Everlasting Father, Prince of Peace.

Group One: He is the King of kings and Lord of lords.

Group Two: The Holy One, the Cornerstone.

Group Three: He is Jesus Christ, the Son of God.

Group Two: He is the Good Shepherd, the Bread of Life.

Group One: He is the Bright Morning Star, the Captain of the Lord's hosts.

Group Three: He is Jesus Christ, the Son of God.

Group Two: Deliverer.

Group One: Lamb of God.

Group Two: Savior.

Group One: Holy One of Israel.

Group Three: He is Jesus Christ, the Son of God.

Group One: King of glory.

Group Two: Light of the World.

Group Three: He is Jesus Christ, the Son of God.

Group One: From everlasting,

Group Two: To everlasting,

All: He is Jesus Christ, the Son of God.

Digging Deeper
- Which name of Jesus do you like most? Why?
- Which name of Jesus helps you remember that Jesus is God's Son? Why?

Puppy Love

Scripture
John 14:23

Props
none

Characters
Trainer
Jeff
Fluffy

Scene Setup
Ask some/all of the children to form pairs and decide which member of each pair is "heads" and which is "tails." Tell children who are "tails" that they now have them: they're to play the roles of puppies and their partners will be their owners.

Ask the children playing puppies to get on their hands and knees. Ask them to practice three commands: sit, beg, and shake hands.

Say, "Puppy obedience school isn't for wimps. The puppies work hard, the owners work hard, and if everything goes right, the graduation ceremony is a time of celebration. Here at the Attaboy School of Puppy Obedience it's graduation day—and you're all doing very well. The puppies are obeying, the owners are cooperating, and all is well—except for Jeff and Fluffy."

Script

Trainer: I want to congratulate all of you. You've completed the obedience course and after this final test you will receive your diplomas. But first, as Head Trainer of the Attaboy School of Puppy Obedience, it's my honor to ask all puppies to face their owners. [*indicate that the "puppies" should do so*] Now, Sit!

Fluffy *shakes* Jeff's *hand*

Jeff: No, Fluffy! You're supposed to be sitting, not shaking hands.

Trainer: Having a problem there, Jeff?

Jeff: No, Head Trainer. Fluffy just got a bit confused. Must be the pressure of the graduation.

Trainer: Very well. Then puppies, Beg!

Fluffy *sits*

Jeff: Fluffy, you want to flunk this test? Beg, Fluffy, Beg!

Trainer: Jeff, it appears your puppy isn't ready to graduate.

Jeff: One more chance, Head Trainer. Please.

Trainer: Well, okay. But just one. Puppies, Shake Hands.

Jeff: Fluffy, if you love me, please obey my command. Shake hands, Fluffy!

Fluffy *stands up and shakes* Jeff's *hand, claps him on the back, gives him a big hug*

Trainer: What a performance! Fluffy, Jeff—you graduate first in your class!

Jeff: Wonderful! That's great!

Fluffy: Woof! Woof!

Digging Deeper

๛ When you love others, are you more likely to do what they want you to do? Why or why not?

๛ Why do you think Jesus makes a point of telling us that if we love him, we'll obey him?

๛ What's one way you've obeyed Jesus in the past week?

Disappearing Act

Scripture
John 10:25

Props
glass half full of water
coin
five-dollar bill

Characters
Marvin
Margaret
Emily

Scene Setup
Place *Marvin* in the front of the performance area, and let *Margaret* and *Emily* sit on the floor with some/all of the children. Give the five-dollar bill to *Margaret*. Give the rest of the props to *Marvin*.

Say, "Someone gave Marvin a do-it-yourself card trick book and ever since he's been trying to dazzle his friends with magic tricks. This is his first real magic show. And if it goes badly, it will probably be his last."

Script

Marvin: Ladies and gentlemen, boys and girls, welcome to the greatest show on earth!

Margaret: That's a pretty big introduction for a backyard magic show.

Emily: Marvin's been working on his act.

Margaret: I hope so. Everybody here paid twenty-five cents to see it.

Marvin: You, Ma'am—please take this coin and lay it flat in your hand. [Marvin *hands coin to* Emily] Do not let me see which side of the coin is facing up. Are you ready?

Emily: All set.

Marvin: Tell me—which side is facing up.

Emily: Heads.

Marvin: Exactly right! I could tell by reading your mind! Please return the quarter to me.

Margaret: Hey! What kind of trick was that?

Marvin: You want to see something truly amazing? Behold—I shall make this cup of water disappear! [*turns his back to the crowd and drinks the water, then turns*] Ta-dah!

Margaret: Lame! That was lame!

Marvin: Now I shall make something more solid disappear. Who here has a five-dollar bill?

Margaret: I do.

Emily: Where did you get a five-dollar bill?

Margaret: It's my birthday money.

Marvin: May I have it, please? [Margaret *hands it to* Marvin] Thank you, Ma'am.

Margaret: You'd better be careful with that, Marvin!

Marvin: Now, if you will all clap your hands three times, you'll see this five-dollar bill disappear before your very eyes.

Margaret, Emily, *and the rest of the children clap three times*

Marvin: Bye-bye. [*runs from room*]

Margaret: Hey! Come back here with my money! [Margaret *gets up and runs after him*]

Digging Deeper

- The Amazing Marvin tried to trick people into thinking he could do the impossible. How did Jesus perform miracles?
- When people saw Jesus perform miracles, how do you think they felt?
- Where do you think Jesus got his power to be truly amazing?

Diamond Double

Scripture
Deuteronomy 4:39

Props
none

Characters
Auctioneer
Mrs. Devore
Mr. Smith

Scene Setup
Place some/all of the children in rows, with *Mrs. Devore* and *Mr. Smith* among them. Say, "Welcome to the very exclusive Auction House of Channelle Louise, where only the most exotic items are put up for auction. This is where last year a painting by Michelangelo sold for 14 million dollars. Today an even rarer item is up for sale. Don't raise your hand or the *Auctioneer* will think you want to pay for the item in front of you. Ladies and gentlemen, behold the rarest gem in the world—the 2-pound Ontario Diamond. It is so clear and perfect you can't even see it! Let's join the auction."

———— Script ————

Auctioneer: Ladies and gentlemen, this famous diamond was found in a rare Canadian diamond mine, then cut and polished by the best craftsmen in the world. It has been owned by the royal family of Lamdoola, but is now, for the very first time, available for purchase. Our bidding will begin at 20 million dollars.

Mrs. Devore: What a beautiful jewel! I simply must have it for my collection!

Mr. Smith: Even at 20 million dollars it's a bargain. There's no other diamond like it anywhere!

Mrs. Devore: I bid 21 million dollars.

Mr. Smith: And I raise the bid to 22 million dollars.

Auctioneer: The high bid stands at 22 million dollars. Does anyone wish to bid more?

Mrs. Devore: I raise my bid to 25 million dollars, plus I'll throw in my very expensive handbag.

Mr. Smith: Oh yeah? I'll bid 25 million dollars, a very expensive handbag, and my car.

Mrs. Devore: I'll bid all that and also throw in my chauffeur.

Auctioneer: Madam, I'm afraid we can't take a chauffeur as part of your payment.

Mrs. Devore: Why not? He's in good health!

Auctioneer: Because to do so would mean—wait a moment, please. I've just been handed a note. An incredible event has just happened! It seems the Canadian diamond mine that produced this diamond has uncovered another diamond just as big. A diamond just as beautiful!

Mr. Smith: Well, in that case, drop my bid to twenty-five bucks.

Mrs. Devore: Forget my bid altogether. Who wants a diamond that isn't one-of-a-kind?

Mr. Smith: Good point. Look, I'll give you ten dollars to take it off your hands, but I want it gift wrapped.

Mr. Smith: Going, going, gone. Sold for ten dollars!

Digging Deeper

- If there are a lot of copies of a painting, they aren't worth much. If there's just one, it is considered very valuable. Why do you think this is so?
- There is only one true God. Why does that make knowing him so important?
- Because there's only one true God, what does that mean in your life?

Scripture
Mark 16:15, 20

Props
newspaper
chair
crown

Characters
King
Loyal Servant

Scene Setup
Place the *King* on a chair in the center of the performance area, facing the children. In the *King's* hands is a newspaper, open and hiding his face. The *Loyal Servant* stands nearby.

Say, "It's been a hard year here in the kingdom of Limilock. It is now the dead of winter in the year 1340. The crops failed last spring. The cows and sheep died last summer. And the sheriff just raised your taxes. You're an angry, starving mob of peasants, gathered outside the royal palace. You expect the king to come out onto the palace balcony to share some good news and give you hope. If you hear something you like, you'll erupt with applause and shouts of approval. Here sits your king. He's well fed, wearing warm clothes, and living in a palace. And here's his loyal servant."

Script

Loyal Servant: Your Majesty, there is a mob of starving peasants outside in the courtyard.

King: Have the Captain of the Guard throw them out.

Loyal Servant: The Captain of the Guard is a starving peasant, Sire. So are all the guards.

King: Then ignore them. Maybe they'll go away.

Loyal Servant: But there are thousands of them, Sire. And they're about to break in here, grab us, burn the place to the ground, then stab you with swords, spears, pitchforks, and other pointy things. Maybe you should go tell them some good news?

King: I'm busy.

Loyal Servant: But someone needs to tell them good news, Sire.

King: Then do it yourself.

Loyal Servant: [*reading a few lines of the newspaper over the* King's *shoulder*] Let's see. There was a story about—here it is! [*dashing over to announce loudly to crowd*] There will be bread and meat distributed for free tomorrow down by the moat! [*the mob roars with approval,* Loyal Servant *scampers back and reads a few more lines of the newspaper*] And there was another story, too. Let's see. There it is! [*dashing over to announce loudly to crowd*] The royal buggy-whip factory is hiring more workers so you can earn money to buy houses and clothing! [*the mob roars with approval,* Loyal Servant *scampers back and reads a few more lines out of the newspaper, then dashes over to the balcony to announce loudly*] And our national soccer team won last night! [*mob roars with approval*] I think they're feeling more hopeful, Sire.

King: Good for them.

Loyal Servant: Your Majesty, a humble question. Why didn't *you* tell them the good news?

King: I called the paper and they printed the good news. People can read it for themselves.

Loyal Servant: But they're starving peasants, Sire. Some of them can't read. Some can't afford a paper. And starving people don't stop to read, Sire.

King: Go get me another cup of hot chocolate or you'll be a starving peasant, too!

Loyal Servant: Yes, Your Majesty. Right away, Sire!

Loyal Servant *scampers off the stage*

Digging Deeper

~ How was the king like us when it comes to sharing the Good News about Jesus?

~ Is it a good idea to count on people reading about Jesus in the Bible for themselves? Why or why not?

~ Name someone you know who needs to hear the Good News about Jesus.

It Only Takes One

Scripture
Acts 4:12

Props
football

Characters
Coach
Johnson
Smith
Jed

Scene Setup
Arrange some/all of the children in a loose huddle formation around the *Coach*. Place *Johnson* and *Smith* in the huddle, place *Jed* in a corner at the other end of the performance area.

Say, "The football game is about to begin, and it's team huddle time. The coach has a few words to say, so listen close."

Script

Coach: Okay, team, I won't try to sugarcoat this. We're in trouble. I know you've prepared hard. You want to win this one. But I'll be honest—I don't think that's going to happen.

Smith: Excuse me, Coach, but isn't this supposed to be a pep talk?

Johnson: You know, where you focus on the positives?

Coach: That's what I'm doing, Johnson. These are the positives.

Johnson: Ouch. We are in trouble.

Coach: I owe it to you to be realistic, and I've seen the game films. Read the scouting reports. Run the numbers. You guys are going to be lucky to get out alive.

Smith: What's the other team got that we don't?

Coach: There's raw power; you aren't even going to slow that team down. And focus. And speed. And purpose. And strategy. You want me to go on?

Johnson: Maybe we can run some special plays?

Smith: Or cheat?

Coach: Maybe we can just surrender now and save your lives. [*checks wristwatch*] Well, time to go face the music. Line up here.

Smith: Wait a second, Coach. Who's that big guy? He's coming this way!

Coach: I'll be a potbellied hamster. We're saved!

Johnson: Did you think of some great new play? Some amazing strategy to help us win?

Coach: You? You're not even going to play. As a matter of fact, I'm not going to coach!

Smith: Then how are we saved?

Coach: [*pointing in the direction of the "big guy"*] He's gonna save us. He'll play the game for us, and he'll win.

Johnson: You're kidding! And you think he can beat the other team by himself?

Coach: I don't just think it, son. I'm sure of it.

Digging Deeper

- Jesus is the only one who can "win the game." How do you get on his team?

- What are you scared of? How can Jesus save you from it?

- As you serve Jesus, who stands against you?

Have a Heart

Scripture
John 4:1-41

Props
table

Characters
Randy
Dr. Smith
Dr. Jones

Scene Setup
Have *Randy* lie down face up on a table and place *Drs. Jones* and *Smith* behind the table standing over him. Gather some/all of the children in a group (seated or standing, depending on the size of your group) on the other side of the table. You've just created an operating room.

Say, "One of the best things about being in medical school, as you all are, is watching operations. You're gathered to witness Dr. Jones and Dr. Smith do an open-heart surgery on Randy. Because of a new technique, the surgery is totally painless, so Randy is completely awake. He can talk, but he can't move."

Script

Randy: Dr. Smith, you're absolutely sure you know what you're doing?

Dr. Smith: Young man, I've been doing this surgery for twenty years. You're in good hands.

Randy: How about Dr. Jones there?

Dr. Smith: He has plenty of experience, too. And by letting us operate in front of these medical students, they'll get valuable experience, also.

Dr. Jones: Students, you'll see we've opened up the chest cavity and have spread the subject's ribs.

Randy: Randy. The subject's name is Randy.

Dr. Jones: Oh, so sorry. I keep forgetting you're awake.

Randy: Let's try to keep me awake, okay?

Dr. Jones: Certainly. Now students, note the tissue here on the left side of the heart. It appears our initial plan to simply repair it isn't going to work after all.

Randy: What? Why not?

Dr. Jones: Well, young man, it appears the oxidation and sub-clavial ostomosis has—

Randy: Just give it to me straight, Doc.

Dr. Smith: You're going to die. Any minute now.

Randy: Not that straight! Isn't there anything you can do?

Dr. Smith: Well, your heart looks like someone left it in the microwave too long. You're a goner, no doubt about it. Sorry.

Randy: But, but—

Dr. Jones: There is one possibility.

Randy: Just name it, Doc!

Dr. Jones: If one of these students would donate his or her heart, it might work as a transplant. Of course, it would kill the student who donated it. And we have to do the surgery in the next few minutes before you croak.

Randy: Hey, guys. Have a heart. I mean, I mean . . . won't someone give me a heart?

Digging Deeper

ﻌ Is there anyone you would willingly die for?

ﻌ Why do you think Jesus chose to die for you? How does that make you feel?

ﻌ What's one way this week you can love someone as Jesus loves you?

What Would Jesus Do?

Scripture
1 Peter 1:15

Props
chairs
WWJD bracelet

Characters
Mr. Bob
Josiah
Officer Greg

Scene Setup
Arrange some/all of the children as if they're seated in a church bus. Place *Mr. Bob* in the driver's seat, *Josiah* in the back of the bus, and *Officer Greg* at the back of the performance area.

Say, "Your entire Bible school class is on a trip to Water World. Mr. Bob is your special guest, mostly because he knows how to drive the church bus. You were supposed to leave the parking lot at 7:30, but a couple kids were late so you didn't actually pull out until 7:45. Mr. Bob is trying to make up for lost time by driving fast. Put on your seat belt and join the crowd!"

Script

Mr. Bob: Don't worry kids—we'll get to Water World before the gates open!

Josiah: I just hope we get there alive! This bus must be going one hundred miles an hour!

Mr. Bob: No way, Josiah. We're not going a bit over ninety. Just hang onto your seats!

Josiah: But aren't you speeding, Mr. Bob?

Mr. Bob: Let's just say we're going 55 miles an hour with tremendous enthusiasm.

Josiah: Mr. Bob, what would Jesus do if he were late? Would he break the law to make up for lost time?

Mr. Bob: Jesus didn't have an old church bus, Josiah, so I guess we'll never know.

Josiah: Umm, Mr. Bob, maybe you should pull over.

Mr. Bob:	No reason to. I checked the oil and tire pressure before we left.
Josiah:	Yeah, but there's a police car right behind us, and his lights are on.
Mr. Bob:	Oh, bother.

Officer Greg *comes up alongside the bus and stands looking at* Mr. Bob

Mr. Bob:	Good day, Officer! Lovely day for our church group to go to Water World, isn't it?
Officer Greg:	Yes, sir. May I see your license and registration, please? [Mr. Bob *pretends to hand papers to* Officer Greg] Do you have any idea how fast you were going back there, sir?
Mr. Bob:	Ohh . . . a little over 55. But how fast could this old bus go?
Officer Greg:	I clocked you going ninety-two miles an hour. I'll have to give you a ticket, sir.
Mr. Bob:	Are you sure about that radar reading, Officer?
Officer Greg:	Yes, I am. And sir, what's that bracelet you're wearing?
Mr. Bob:	Glad you noticed, Officer. It says WWJD. All of us are wearing one because that's what we ask when we make decisions—"What would Jesus do?" Ask yourself that question, Officer. You've pulled over a bus full of joyful Christians on the way to Water World for a time of fellowship. What would Jesus do? Let us go, right?
Officer Greg:	Sir, please think of that bracelet as standing for "Water World Just got Delayed," because you're not going anywhere right now. I think it's going to take me a little bit of time to write up this ticket. I'm not in any hurry.

Digging Deeper

2 Did Mr. Bob's actions honor God's holiness?

2 What does it mean to live a holy life? Give some examples.

2 How would this skit be different if Mr. Bob had decided to live a holy life regarding his driving?

2 What's an area of your life where you find it difficult to live a holy life?

Busy Beaver Baloney

Scripture
Galatians 5:22, 23

Props
cellophane tape
markers
paper

Characters
Troop Leader
Jessie
Ashley

Scene Setup
Ahead of time design four merit badges to place on Jessie: badges for "humility," "patience," "gentleness," and "self-control."

Give each child two small pieces of paper (2-by-2-inch squares work well) and a marker. Ask children to quickly design merit badges for the two character traits they most wish they had. The badges can be a word or a simple picture. When the children have finished, tape the badges on them. Tape the extra badges you prepared on Jessie. Place some/all of the children in a semicircle around Jessie.

Say, "Welcome to the Troop Meeting of the Busy Beavers, Troop 101. Tonight we're celebrating the presentation of merit badges."

Script

Troop Leader:	Before we close our meeting tonight, I want to congratulate Jessie Smith, who earned more merit badges this month than any other Busy Beaver. Jessie, would you like to say a few words to encourage the other Busy Beavers?
Jessie:	Thanks, Troop Leader. You know, anyone could win this many badges in one month. Of course, that person would need my looks, talent, and smarts. And as I look around this circle I see that nobody else here is nearly as good-looking, talented, or smart as I am. So I guess none of you losers will ever be able to match my record!
Ashley:	Excuse me—
Jessie:	Hey, I'm not finished with my speech yet!

Ashley: But didn't you just get merit badges for "humility" and "self-control"?

Jessie: Sure did—they're right here, you bonehead.

Ashley: But you aren't acting very humble. Or showing much self-control.

Jessie: Hey, I'm humble and self-controlled and I've got the badges to prove it. Like it's any of your business.

Troop Leader: Now, now . . .

Jessie: Wait your turn, Old Timer. I've got a badge for "patience," but that doesn't mean I'm going to let you interrupt me.

Ashley: You see? Just doing a few good deeds and pinning on a badge doesn't mean you really have all those great character traits.

Jessie: Yeah? Well, I don't need this stupid club. I'm out of here. I'm gonna go join a cooler club. One that really appreciates me. Maybe the Marines!

Jessie stomps off stage

Digging Deeper

- What character traits did you put on your badges? Why did you choose those?
- How does someone develop a character trait like those you chose?
- How do you know when someone is patient, humble, or self-controlled?

Worship Resources

Each of the skits in this book correlates to a unit of worship from Standard Publishing's two-year series of Worship Folders for elementary kids. The worship series was developed to help children worship God for who he is and what he has done. Each eight-page folder is a thematic unit with Scripture activities, music, prayer suggestions, and small group ideas for four sessions of children's worship.

Listed with each skit title below is the correlating Worship Folder and its order number.

Exhibit #101
God Is Creator (42241)

Broken Promises
God Is a Promise Keeper (42247)

Table Talk
God Is Our Caregiver (42248)

Double Identity
Jesus Is Immanuel (42251)

Believe It or Not!
Jesus Is God's Son (42252)

Who's the Loser?
Jesus Is Our Friend (42246)

Make a Run for It!
God Is Forgiving (42243)

Dying to Get Out of Here
Jesus Is Alive (42255)

Good Vibrations
Jesus Is Our Shepherd (42249)

Hangin' Out
God Is Sovereign (42250)

How Long Is Forever?
God Is Eternal (42244)

Hope Strikes Out
Jesus Is Our Hope (42256)

Follow the Leader
God Is Ever-Present (42245)

Winner Takes All
God Is Powerful (42242)

He's All Ears
God Is All-Knowing (42254)

Jesus, Name Above All Names
Jesus Is Messiah (42257)

Puppy Love
Jesus Is Our Teacher (42258)

Disappearing Act
Jesus, Miracle Doer (42259)

Diamond Double
God, the Only God (42260)

No News Is Bad News
Jesus Is Good News (42261)

It Only Takes One
Jesus Is Savior (42253)

Have a Heart
Jesus Is Love (42262)

What Would Jesus Do?
God Is Holy (42263)

Busy Beaver Baloney
God Is Inside Us (42264)